LOUISIANA ANIMALS ABC

By Rickey Pittman

Illustrated by Kay Meadows

PELICAN PUBLISHING
New Orleans 2022

"No matter how few possessions you own or how little money you have, loving wildlife and nature will make you rich beyond measure."
—Paul Oxton, founder, Wild Heart Wildlife Foundation

ISBN 9781455626731
E-book ISBN 9781455626748

Printed in Korea

Published by Pelican Publishing
New Orleans, LA
www.pelicanpub.com

From Louisiana's northern
   piney woods
To the bayou's winding mysteries,
From the coastlines to the beaches
To the Cameron Parish prairies,
From the marshes and the lakes
To the parks in the cities,
Animals make their homes.

Louisiana's two million alligators
Live in bayous, marshes, or lakes.
They lay their eggs in August
In mud mounds the female makes.

A

The longest alligator ever caught in Louisiana measured 19 feet, 2 inches long. That was way back in 1890!

The alligator snapping turtle
Attracts fish in a strange way.
Wiggling its tongue like a worm,
It hunts throughout the day.

The alligator snapping turtle can bite through a broom handle! It is considered a restricted harvest species, meaning that licensed recreational fishermen can only take one per day.

Bats find food in the dark
By use of reflected sound waves.
The only flying mammal,
They roost in trees and caves.

Echolocation: Locating objects using sonar or reflected sound. Bats control harmful insect populations while also helping to pollinate certain plants. Bats in Louisiana do not bite humans for their blood.

The black bear is Louisiana's state mammal.
Adaptable with a long-term memory,
They hibernate in winter
To conserve their strength and energy.

Louisiana black bears are a protected species. They live mostly in forests throughout the lower Mississippi River Valley.

President Teddy Roosevelt, who loved to hunt, once declined to shoot a bear tied to a tree. An artist drew that scene and the Teddy bear stuffed toy was created.

Crawfish can live for up to thirty years!
Louisiana's official crustacean,
They walk backward but swim forward
In ponds and the Atchafalaya River Basin.

Crawfish are also called "crawdads," "crayfish," and "mudbugs," and many Louisiana festivals celebrate the popular crustacean.

C

Coyotes are known to be wily;
You hear their howls at night.
Catahoulas sport a spotted coat—
Black, brown, gray, and white.

Coyotes mate for life. They are considered pests that carry diseases and are often a danger to small pets.

The Catahoula Leopard Dog is Louisiana's state dog.

Dolphins are intelligent mammals
Who like to hunt for fish.
You can see a rare pink dolphin
In the waters of Calcasieu Parish.

The hunting of white-tailed deer
Is carefully managed by law.
Whether fawn, buck, or doe,
We must preserve them all.

Twenty-six breeds of dragonflies and damselflies,
Make their home in Louisianne.
With eyes that can see in all directions,
It's good luck if they land on your hand.

Also called mosquito hawks, dragonflies make a basket with their feet to catch prey in the air and will eat while flying.

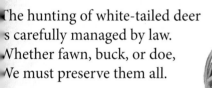

Several types of ducks—whistling ducks, wood ducks, teal, pintail, ring-necked, coots, mallards, and others—winter in Louisiana. They come in a variety of colors and plumage. Some are dabblers while others are diving ducks.

The bald eagle's Volkswagen-sized nests
Can be seen in the Atchafalaya River Basin.
Eagles have greatly increased in number,
A success story of conservation.

Legal protections and banning the use of DDT pesticide saved the bald eagle from extinction. In 1960, Louisiana had only four eagle nests. Now there are hundreds! Morgan City in St. Mary Parish celebrates the eagle every year with an Eagle Expo. They offer boat tours, raptor demonstrations, and guest speakers.

Egrets have an S-shaped neck
And silently glide through the air.
Cattle egrets perch on the back of cows,
But to see them in flocks is rare.

Egrets were once hunted nearly to extinction for their feathers, which were used to decorate ladies' hats.

The American bullfrog's croak
Is loud and deep at night.
It is how he calls to females
While giving other males a fright.

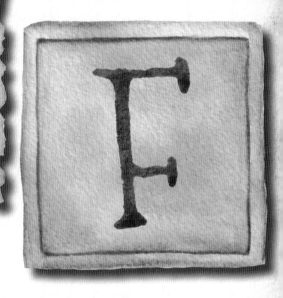

American bullfrogs are the largest frogs in
North America and can jump nearly six feet.
A group of frogs is called an army.
There are more than thirty species of frogs in
Louisiana, including American toads, the Cajun
chorus frog, the threatened crawfish frog, and the
invasive Cuban tree frog.

The red fox and the gray fox
Can make forty different sounds.
Valued for hunting mice and rats,
They make burrows in the ground.

Baby foxes are called kits or pups.
Foxes can climb trees and have amazing
hearing. It's been said that they can
hear the ticking of a watch from forty
yards away! They are also playful and
have been known to steal golf balls. Fox
fur is considered very valuable.

Louisiana has four species of gar,
But the alligator gar wins in size.
Gar are as old as the dinosaurs
But are so difficult to clean, their meat is no prize!

G

The four gar species in Louisiana's waters are the longnose gar, the shortnose gar, the alligator gar, and the spotted gar. Alligator gar can grow up to ten feet in length and weigh three hundred pounds! In Louisiana, gar are often prepared by making fried gar balls, but getting to the meat is an effort, because they are so hard to clean.

G is for gaspergou, a tasty freshwater drum.
When caught on a line, they put up a fight!
Their "lucky bones" help the fish balance,
And their eyes reflect light at night.

The ear bones of the gaspergou received the nickname of "lucky bones" because they have an L-shaped groove on them. In each eye, gaspergou have a layer of cells that gathers and reflects light. That reflection is easy to see in the light of a camera's flash or a flashlight at night.

eral hogs are a nuisance
rought here by the Spanish.
hey damage crops and food for deer;
Ve wish they all would vanish!

Wild hogs can be found in all sixty-four of Louisiana's parishes. They damage food sources for other animals, destroy crops, and contribute to erosion.

Audubon painted the
tricolored heron
That bows to its children
in greeting.
Gracefully running,
turning, and spinning,
It eats crabs and shrimp
when feeding.

H

Herons on the Bayou is the largest public art project in Northeast Louisiana and includes fifty heron statues painted by thirty-seven different artists. These seven-foot-tall statues can be found throughout Monroe and West Monroe.

rnithologist (bird
xpert) John James
udubon spent the
mmer of 1821 at
e Oakley House in
. Francisville. Now
own as the Audubon
ate Historic Site, here
udubon created many
the detailed bird
intings for which he is
mous.

A hornet sting contains five times the poison of a wasp's sting. They live in football-shaped nests and tend to attack in groups.

mmingbirds can hover and fly backwards,
d they migrate long distances.
netimes they use spider webs as
ilding materials for their nests.

The white ibis has a very long beak,
A three-foot wingspan, and light blue eyes.
It likes to eat crabs and crawfish
And flies in V formation through the skies.

I

The indigo snake has powerful jaws
And is known to kill its prey
By dashing it against nearby objects.
It eats every other day.

The eastern indigo is the
longest snake in our nation. It is
considered a threatened species
and is protected by law. Once
it ranged from Louisiana to
Georgia, but it has disappeared
from many states, including
Louisiana. Its deep blue color
gives it its name.

The blue jay can imitate
The cries of other birds.
It hides its food, can mob an owl,
And even mimics human words!

Naked as a jaybird
Describes a little baby;
Noisy as a jaybird
Describes a chatty lady!

Blue jays are territorial and can be aggressive. They hold nuts with their feet and crack them with their sharp beaks. They can imitate the cries of hawks.

J

Louisiana has jumping spiders
That can learn to jump on command.
They are by nature curious
And may jump up on your hand!

Jumping spiders don't use webs to catch their prey but ambush by pouncing on it. They have amazing eyesight because they have four pairs of eyes! They attract mates by dancing and singing. If another male is nearby, they may have a dance contest! Some people capture jumping spiders and keep them in a terrarium.

The killdeer is a shorebird
Named for its call, they say.
It can fake a broken wing
To lure predators away.

During nesting season,
a mother killdeer may
pretend to have a broken
wing to lure predators
away from her nest.

K

Louisiana has katydids
That can predict fall weather.
On July summer evenings,
They sing their song together.

Skilled in the art of camouflage, katydids don't usually fly. They may
flutter to the ground but will climb back into the trees. They form
singing groups that loudly chorus "katy-did-katy-didn't." It is said
their night songs were so loud that it frightened the first Pilgrims!

Louisiana has many types of lizards:
Horned, racerunner, house gecko, and glass.
The skink, the prairie, and green anole—
They all can move very fast!

Lizards often lie in the sun to keep warm and to
absorb vitamin D. The body temperatures of these
cold-blooded reptiles are only as warm as the air
around them. Many lizards lose their tail when
grabbed by a predator, but the tail will regenerate.
Some lizards wave their tails to attract spiders and
other insects to eat.

L

Lightning bugs, seen on summer nights,
Are also called glowworms or fireflies.
Producing flashing lights in many colors,
They illuminate Louisiana's dark skies.

While flying, the male lightning bug uses flashing light
patterns to attract mates. Females wait on the ground and
show interest by flashing only once. Fireflies use luciferase,
a light-producing enzyme, to create the chemical reaction
that powers their light.

The Loup Garou is the
mythical Cajun werewolf also
called the Rougarou.

Muskrats are trapped in Louisiana
As a source of money.
They eat a third of their weight in vegetation each day;
The damage they do is not funny!

Millions of muskrat, mink, and nutria pelts are harvested every year in Louisiana. Muskrats can hold their breath under water for longer than ten minutes and can even swim backwards.

In trees and on telephone wires,
You can see the mourning dove.
Its call is sad and lamenting
When pining for its love.

An abundant game bird in North America, mourning doves can drink brackish water. They feed their young "pigeon milk" secreted from the crop (food storage pouch) of the parent bird.

Nutrias escaped from Avery Island,
And now destroy the marsh.
They eat the roots of plants
And the damage is very harsh!

In other countries, nutria are known as coypu. They have orange teeth and eat so much vegetation that they cause soil erosion. Some Louisiana parishes have placed a $5 bounty on each nutria tail collected. Nutria have overtaken muskrat to become the top fur producer in the state.

Nightjars are birds that love the night,
When the whip-poor-will sings.
Nighthawks hunt at dawn and at dusk,
Twisting and flapping their wings.

Opossum ancestors lived during the age of the dinosaurs.
Maybe that's when they learned to play dead.
It's true that they "play possum"—
When the predator looks away, the possum has fled.

An opossum has fifty
teeth in his mouth.
That's a toothy grin!

Today they are only found in Texas,
But the ocelot once roamed our state.
The "little leopard" can rotate its ankles completely around;
What an awesome trait!

The ocelot's tail
is half the length
of its body. It can
also turn its ankles
so that it can
climb down a tree
headfirst instead of
tail first.

The brown pelican is our state bird,
A resident along the Gulf shore.
It's found on the state quarter, flag, and seals,
And once on flags of war.

A pelican dives into water,
Scooping fish up with its beak.
They always fly in a V formation—
A very efficient technique.

Once critically endangered due to pollution and the pesticide DDT, the brown pelican had virtually disappeared from Louisiana. Reintroduced in the 1970s, the species has made a remarkable comeback in the "Pelican State." Many sports teams in Louisiana, such as the New Orleans professional basketball team, are named after the state bird.

On private and public land
Conservationists work to grow
Quail population and habitat
So that future numbers won't be so low.

A group of quail is called a covey,
And together they roost and feed.
A nest of quail eggs is called a clutch;
Quails mate for life to breed.

Bobwhite quails call, "bob-white, bob-white!"
The population of quail in Louisiana has
declined by 75 percent since the 1960s, mainly
due to habitat loss.

Swamp rabbits prefer wet areas
Like a riverbank, marsh, or bog.
They will swim to escape from predators
Or dive underneath a log.

Swamp rabbits are the largest of the cottontail breeds. Their cinnamon-colored fur is so thick, it provides waterproof protection from the water, and they have webbed feet for swimming.

R

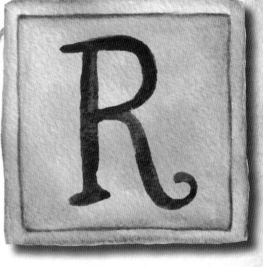

Louisiana has three types of rattlesnakes—
The pygmy, timber, and diamondback.
They make a rattling sound when approached;
If encountered, change your track!

The timber rattler is also called a canebrake rattler.

If you come upon a skunk,
It can lift its tail and spray
A distance of ten feet.
So you better stay away!

S

Squirrels in Louisiana
May be red like a fox, black, or gray.
Some of them can even fly!
Watch them glide and play.

Gray squirrels are often called cat squirrels.
There are three types of squirrels in Louisiana:
eastern gray, fox and southern flying squirrels.
All squirrels love to eat pecans!

Louisiana is blessed with twenty-five species
Of tortoise, turtle, and terrapin.
Some are on an endangered list
Because they are sought by fishermen.

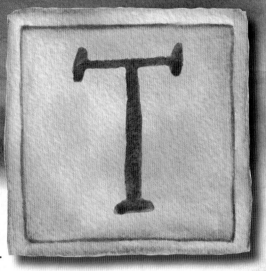

A wild turkey has at least 5,000
feathers,
Used to fly swiftly over the ground.
They swagger and fan their tails;
A gobble is their signature sound.

A poult is a turkey chick. A young male turkey is
called a jake and an adult male is called a tom or a
gobbler. A female is a hen.

The upland sandpiper,
Which the Cajuns call *papabotte,*
Sings a ghostly whistle
From deep down in his throat.

They like the short grass of the prairie
And migrate to the warm sun of the South.
They often perch on fence posts
With a cricket in their mouth.

U

A peep is a nickname for the
smallest of the sandpiper species.

Louisiana has two vultures:
The turkey and the black.
They often roost together,
Watching for a snack!

Vultures ride air currents,
Soaring in graceful flight.
They are usually found in groups,
Especially at night.

According to an old legend, the city of Carencro acquired its name from the site of a large flock of black buzzards or vultures that swarmed over the Vermilion River to feast on a fish die-off. In Cajun French, the word for "buzzard" means "carrion crow."

Wasps won't build a nest
On a light blue painted ceiling.
Legends say insects think it's the sky
That the porch is revealing.

This color of blue paint is called "dirt dauber blue" or "haint blue." Many houses in the New Orleans area use this paint on porch ceilings. Some claim the color also repels ghosts!

W

In the marsh, you might see a sly weasel
Or a woodpecker if you search.
And sometimes when you're fishing,
You may catch a nice white perch!

Once nearly lost to extinction, whooping cranes have been reintroduced in small numbers to Louisiana.
White perch are also called *sac-á-lait* or crappie.

Xenartha is a class of animals
That includes the armadillo,
Who with his flexible armor
Is shaped like a little round pillow.

The nine-banded armadillo's
Baby is called a pup.
A nuisance, they visit yards and gardens
At night and dig them up.

Nine-banded armadillos are most active at
night. In their burrows, they can sleep for up
to sixteen hours at a time! Most of their diet
is made up of insects and larvae.

Colorful yellowjackets
Can give you painful stings.
You can always recognize them
By their pretty yellow rings!

Yellowjackets, unlike honeybees, do not lose their stinger so they can sting again and again. They usually build their nests underground or in the hollows of trees, and they feed on many types of nuisance insects.

Y

The yellow-crowned night-heron
Hides in swamps for safety reasons.
In winter he migrates to Mexico,
But returns for shrimp and crawfish seasons!

Z is for the zoo,
Where all these animals can be found.
From A to Z, you can find them there,
See them in real life, and hear their sound.

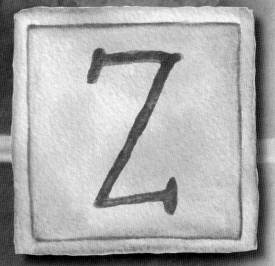

VISIT LOUISIANA ZOOS

Zoos help preserve wildlife
And educate the mind.
Here's a list of some of them;
There's many you can find!

Louisiana Zoos
NEW ORLEANS: Audubon Zoo and
   Audubon Aquarium of the Americas
BROUSSARD: Zoo of Acadiana
ALEXANDRIA: Alexandria Zoological Park
BATON ROUGE: Baton Rouge Zoo
MONROE: Louisiana Purchase Gardens & Zoo

Louisiana State Animals

State Amphibian: Green Tree Frog
State Bird: Eastern Brown Pelican
State Dog: Catahoula Leopard Dog
State Crustacean: Crawfish
State Mammal: Louisiana Black Bear
State Freshwater Fish: White Perch
State Saltwater Fish: Spotted Sea Trout
State Reptile: Alligator
State Insect: Honeybee

Invasive, Pest, and Nuisance Species of Louisiana Animals

nutria
alligator
coyote
feral (wild) hog
Raccoons, opossums, and skunks have become pests due to loss of habitat and have relocated to the suburbs and cities. Raccoons and skunks are known carriers of rabies.
armadillo
Formosan termite
Asian tiger mosquito
zebra mussel
house mouse
red imported fire ant
boll weevil
Rio Grande cichlid

Cajun Words for Louisiana Animals

English	Cajun
alligator	*cocodrie*
armadillo	*rat de bois*
buzzard	*carencro*
catfish	*barbu*
crawfish	*écrevisse*
deer	*chevreuil*
duck	*canard*
frog	*ouaouaron*
night heron	*grosbec*
owl	*hibou*
pig	*cochon*
possum	*rat de bois*
rabbit	*lapin*
raccoon	*chaouis*
redfish	*poisson rouge*

English	Cajun
shrimp	*cheuvrette*
snake	*serpent*
squirrel	*écureuil*
teal duck	*canard sarcelle*
turtle	*tortue*
white perch	*sac-á-lait*
wood duck	*canard de bois*

Selected Endangered and Protected Louisiana Animals

Whooping Crane
Red-cockaded woodpecker
Louisiana pine snake
Gopher tortoise
Green sea turtle
Leatherback sea turtle
Loggerhead sea turtle
West Indian manatee
Northern long-eared bat